W9-CGY-035

The Nature and Science of
FOSSILS

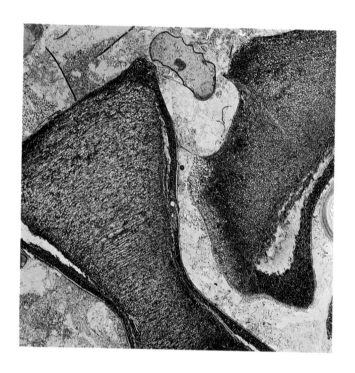

Jane Burton and Kim Taylor

J560
BUR

Gareth Stevens Publishing
MILWAUKEE

For a free color catalog describing Gareth Stevens Publishing's list of high-quality books and multimedia programs, call 1-800-542-2595 (USA) or 1-800-461-9120 (Canada). Gareth Stevens Publishing's Fax: (414) 225-0377.

Library of Congress Cataloging-in-Publication Data

Burton, Jane.
The nature and science of fossils / by Jane Burton and Kim Taylor.
p. cm. — (Exploring the science of nature)
Includes bibliographical references and index.
Summary: Discusses the nature and formation of fossils,
the different types, and how and where to find them.
ISBN 0-8368-2183-1 (lib. bdg.)
1. Fossils—Juvenile literature. [1. Fossils. 2. Paleontology.]
I. Taylor, Kim. II. Title. III. Series: Burton, Jane.
Exploring the science of nature.
QE714.5.B87   1999
560—dc21   98-31770

First published in North America in 1999 by
Gareth Stevens Publishing
1555 North RiverCenter Drive, Suite 201
Milwaukee, Wisconsin 53212 USA

This U.S. edition © 1999 by Gareth Stevens, Inc. Created with original © 1998 by White Cottage Children's Books. Text © 1998 by Kim Taylor. Photographs © 1998 by Jane Burton, Kim Taylor, and Mark Taylor. The photograph on page 9 (below) is courtesy of the Natural History Museum, London. The photographs on pages 8 (above), 12 (below), and 13 (center) are by Jan Taylor. Conceived, designed, and produced by White Cottage Children's Books, 29 Lancaster Park, Richmond, Surrey TW10 6AB, England. Additional end matter © 1999 by Gareth Stevens, Inc.

The rights of Jane Burton and Kim Taylor to be identified as the authors of this work have been asserted by them in accordance with the Copyright, Design and Patents Act 1988. Educational consultant, Jane Weaver; scientific adviser, Dr. Jan Taylor.

All rights to this edition reserved to Gareth Stevens, Inc. No part of this book may be reproduced, stored in a retrieval system, or transmitted in any form or by any means, electronic, mechanical, photocopying, recording, or otherwise without the prior written permission of the publisher except for the inclusion of brief quotations in an acknowledged review.

Printed in the United States of America

1 2 3 4 5 6 7 8 9 03 02 01 00 99

Contents

Turned to Stone 4

Fossil Forms 6

Time to Reflect 10

The Age of Fossils 12

Sea Sediments 14

Devil's Toenails 16

Fossil Wood 18

Crawling on Land 20

Living Fossils 22

Gone Forever 24

Activities: Finding Fossils 28

Glossary 30

Plants and Animals/Books to Read 31

Videos/Web Sites/Index 32

Words that appear in the glossary are printed in **boldface** type the first time they occur in the text.

Turned to Stone

Top: Sharks' teeth are very hard, but their skeletons are soft. All that remains of many prehistoric sharks are their teeth.

Fossils are the remains or traces of dead plants and animals that have turned to stone. To understand how living material can become stone, imagine the body of an animal, such as a fish, sinking slowly into the dark depths of a **prehistoric** ocean.

After days of sinking, the dead fish rests on the fine **silt** at the bottom of the ocean. The water is cold, and darkness is all around. There is great pressure from the water above. The fish's body just lies there.

Storms rage on the surface, and rivers pour more silt into the water. The silt falls through the water like fine snow, in layers, covering the fish. The pressure increases as the layers of silt build up, gradually squashing the fish flat. What remains of the fish is just a skeleton, teeth, and a few scales.

Slow chemical changes take place in the fish's skeleton. The original bone is gradually replaced by **minerals** from the surrounding silt.

The huge amount of pressure from above squeezes out all water from between the silt grains, and the silt becomes rock. Hidden within the rock are the bones of the fish — now turned to stone. A fossil has formed!

Opposite: This little fish died 150 million years ago. Plant-like traces of minerals make the fish look as if it is swimming in seaweed.

Below: The body of this fish, only about 3 inches (7 centimeters) long, has been embedded in rock for 21 million years. The fish's outline and its bones are clearly visible.

Fossil Forms

Top: Squid-like belemnites swarmed in the seas from **Jurassic** to **Cretaceous** times. Their internal shells formed bullet-shaped fossils.

Above: Three bones from the tail of a dinosaur fossilized together.

Most fossils are formed from the hard parts of animals and plants. Bones, teeth, shells, and wood frequently fossilize. Fossils resulting from the soft parts of animals and plants are much rarer. This is because the soft parts usually rot away or are eaten by other animals. Soft material is also easily crushed and may be destroyed by pressure from above as rock forms.

Rare fossils that show the soft parts of animal bodies are found only in certain kinds of rock. Rock formed from very fine mud can sometimes preserve the finest details of animals. But special conditions are needed for these fossils to form. When mud covers an animal's body quickly —

Right: Tower shells trapped in mud 20 million years ago have become hard, white fossils in gray stone.

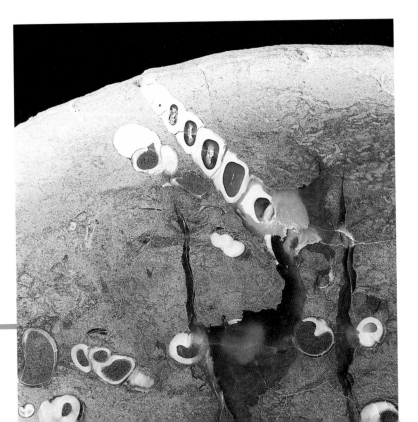

Above: About 3 or 4 million years ago, immense sharks, over 40 feet (12 meters) long, swam in the oceans. Their huge, fossilized teeth prove their existence.

Long ago, animals with paired shells, called brachiopods or lamp shells, were very common. Their fossilized shells occur in vast numbers in some types of rock.

preventing other animals from eating it — minerals start replacing the soft parts at once. The minerals may harden the soft parts of the body sufficiently to prevent them from being destroyed by pressure and other disturbances. Then, there is a chance that a fossil will form.

Below: Time can turn tree trunks into hard stone. When the stone is cut and polished, fine details of the wood can be seen.

A split chunk of **sedimentary** rock reveals a squashed fly. The fly has been embedded in the rock for 25 million years.

Fossils do not always form directly from animals and plants. Some fossils are just **impressions**. A leaf may sink to the muddy bottom of a lake where it becomes covered by a layer of silt. Gradually, it rots away, leaving a leaf-shaped impression in the mud. The silt above is squeezed into the impression, and the material eventually becomes stone. If the stone were to be split open, a perfect leaf shape would be visible. But it is not a fossilized leaf. It is just the fossilized impression of a leaf.

Animal tracks become fossilized in a similar way. It is possible to see how some **extinct** species of animals walked by studying their fossilized tracks. By looking at fossilized footprints, scientists

Above: Sea scorpions scuttled across the sandy bottom of the Devonian oceans, leaving trails behind them. The fossilized trails remain in sandstone rock.

Below: Long ago, the coiled shell of an **ammonite** was embedded in gray mudstone. When the stone was split, the fossil shell itself fell away cleanly, leaving two half impressions in the stone.

Millions of years ago, a leaf fell into the water of a boiling hot spring. Deposits from the water formed all over the leaf. The leaf itself soon rotted away, but its impression remains to this day.

Left: In this illustration, a herd of Apatosauruses wanders across a muddy Cretaceous shore, leaving trails of footprints. If the mud later turned into rock, their prints could someday be visible as fossil impressions.

Below: A 35-million-year-old centipede was perfectly preserved in amber during the **Cenozoic** Era.

have even discovered what the patterns on the soles of some dinosaurs' feet were like.

The fine details of some extinct small animals have been fossilized in another way. Instead of being turned to stone, their entire bodies are preserved in amber. Amber is the fossilized **resin** of ancient plants. The clear, sticky resin oozed from the stems of these plants millions of years ago, and insects and spiders occasionally drowned in it. The bodies of these creatures are now visible, set in the transparent amber.

Time to Reflect

Top: False cockle and turret shells like these from late Cenozoic times may still be fossilizing.

One meaning of the word *reflect* is to think about the days gone by. When we reflect on the past, we may think about what happened last week, last year, or maybe even two thousand years ago when the Romans invaded Europe. To consider time that far back, however, does not even come close to the very early time periods when most of the fossils discovered today were formed.

Right: A fallen tree lies among rocks in a dry part of Africa. The tree is now hard stone and is the fossil of a huge tree that grew there in **Carboniferous** times.

Left: Ten thousand years ago, hairy mammoths, like this one, lived in Europe, Asia, and North America. After their deaths, some of their bodies became frozen in ice. Some complete mammoth bodies have been discovered.

Fossils can take as long as many thousands or even millions of years to form. That is why no scientific experiments can be done to fully understand how fossils form.

Fossils are forming now, in just the same way as they did countless millions of years ago. A few plants and animals that are alive today will turn into fossils millions of years into the future.

Most animals and plants that have lived on Earth disappear completely after their deaths. No trace is ever found of them. Only a few die in places where conditions are right for their remains to become fossilized.

Below: A kingfisher feather lies on wet mud. The feather is unlikely to form a fossil, but it could form an impression if the mud becomes stone millions of years from now.

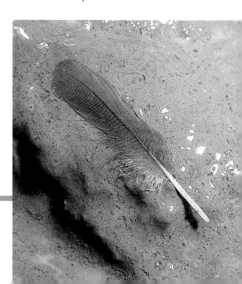

The Age of Fossils

Opposite: There is probably no cliff in the world that contains rock layers from all the periods of prehistoric time. This cliff on the southern coast of England shows rock layers dating from the Jurassic Period.

Below: Fossil stromatolites are the earliest signs of life on Earth, dating from 3.5 billion years ago. They formed when sand and mud became trapped among strands of cyanobacteria.

The oldest fossils on Earth were formed nearly 3.5 billion years ago. They were of simple organisms called **cyanobacteria**. Their fossils formed stone mounds called **stromatolites**.

Animals did not appear on Earth until millions of years later. Some animal species appeared in vast numbers and then died out. Their fossils formed in distinct layers, which **geologists** study to determine the age of rocks. For instance, huge numbers of certain species of ammonites lived in warm, shallow oceans and seawaters during the Jurassic Period (205 to 146 million years ago). Their fossils are found only in Jurassic rocks. Geologists finding layers containing these fossils know that all rocks beneath are older than the Jurassic, and that rocks above are younger. Fossils that play a part in determining the age of rocks are called **index fossils**.

Creatures called **trilobites** are index fossils, especially for the **Cambrian** Period (550 to 510 million years ago). Trilobites lived and died out long before the ammonites. Millions of trilobites, of many different species, swarmed the oceans and seas. They had hard, tough shells, like crab shells, and were easily fossilized. Various species of fossil trilobites are used to identify Cambrian rocks in many different parts of the world.

GEOLOGIC TIME CHART

MILLIONS OF YEARS AGO		
2	CENOZOIC ERA	HUMANS
65	CRETAC-EOUS	
146	JURASSIC	
205	TRIASSIC	
251	PERMIAN	
290	CARBON-IFEROUS	
353	DEVONIAN	
409	SILURIAN	
439	ORDOVI-CIAN	
510	CAMBRIAN	
550		

Sea Sediments

Top: This fossil heart urchin is made of **flint**, but it was found embedded in chalk.

Life on planet Earth began in the oceans, and for millions of years, species developed and multiplied there. Silt from rivers that flowed into the oceans sank to the bottom, forming layer upon layer of **sediment**. Silt was not the only sediment, however. During the Cretaceous Period, fine particles of another kind rained down on the ocean floor. These particles were the shells of tiny sea creatures. The shells were mostly composed of **calcium carbonate**. As layers of these tiny shells built up, chalk rock formed, many feet (meters) thick. Dead sea urchins and sponges were buried in the chalk and fossilized.

Right: The beaches beneath chalk cliffs usually contain huge numbers of flint pebbles. Many of these are the fossilized remains of sponges.

Above: A split lump of flint reveals a perfect heart urchin fossil loosely embedded in it.

The heart urchin fossil can be lifted out because the shell of the urchin has been completely dissolved away.

Fossils in chalk are often formed of flint. Flint is hard and brittle, like glass, and chemically different from chalk.

Where did the flint come from, and how did flint fossils form in chalk? Some of the flint almost certainly came from the sponges themselves. Sponges have soft bodies, sometimes supported by masses of tiny, glassy **spicules** made of **silica**. Silica is the chemical that forms flint, glass, and sand.

During the millions of years that it took for chalk rock to form, the sponge spicules were slowly dissolved by water. The silica filtered into the cavities left by the dead sponges and sometimes inside the hollow shells of sea urchins. This process formed the flint.

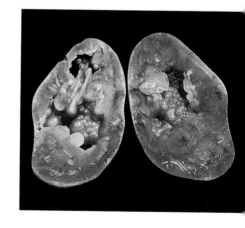

Above: When cut in half, a very ordinary-looking flint pebble turns out to be the fossilized remains of a sponge.

Devil's Toenails

Top: *Devil's toenails* was the name given to these fossil shells.

The shells of living sea snails and **bivalves** are almost as hard as rock. They consist mainly of calcium carbonate, and they readily fossilize. Before scientists knew the origin of fossils, some people named the curly fossil shells that projected from seaside rocks *devil's toenails*.

Some other bivalve shells and the coiled shells of snails have sometimes been pressed together in vast numbers. This process forms a layer of **limestone** rock. When the rock is cut and polished, the fact that it is made of fossilized shells becomes obvious.

Above: A limestone cliff in Western Australia is made of fossilized shell sand.

Right: This Jurassic limestone is packed with the starlike stems of sea lilies. Sea lilies were not flowers, but starfish relatives that attached themselves to the ocean floor.

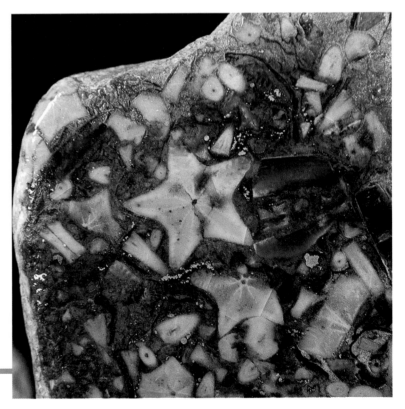

16

Fossil shells make up huge layers of limestone rock, but the fossils have often been so crushed and changed that they are no longer recognizable.

Limestone that has been crushed and heated by movements of the Earth may turn into marble. The Great Pyramids in Egypt — some of the biggest structures ever built — are partly made of rock that was once seashells.

Above: The Great Pyramids in Egypt were built partly of limestone rock.

Fossil Wood

Top: When a fossil log is sliced through and polished, the **growth rings** of the tree can be clearly seen.

Plants and animals lived in the oceans for a very long time before they came out of water onto land. Plants started living on land about 430 million years ago. The first land plants had to find ways to grow successfully on land.

First, they had to form a waterproof outer layer so they would not dry out and shrivel. Secondly, they had to grow rigid stems so they could support themselves on land, rising into the air, instead of just floating in water.

Right: This piece of wood rotted before it became fossilized. Hard, bluish stone formed in the cracks.

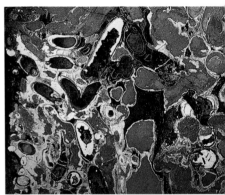

The substance that plants developed to hold themselves upright is wood. Wood is hard and tough. It readily becomes fossilized, and so scientists have been able to study early land plants. Trunks of trees form massive fossils, and even small land plants have woody stems. In some places, whole forests have turned to stone.

Many early land plants belonged to groups that are not very common today. Relatives of plants called club mosses and horsetails once formed forests over 130 feet (40 m) high. When these forests died, thick layers of **peat** sometimes formed. When buried beneath many more layers of sediment, plant matter turned into coal. Coal is the fossilized remains of the vegetation in forests, and that is why it is called a fossil fuel.

Left: Huge chunks of fossilized fir trees lie in an almost desert landscape in Africa. They prove that, in the distant past, the area had plentiful rainfall.

Above: This piece of wood lay in the ocean for years. Shipworms burrowed in it before it fossilized.

Below: Due to pressure and heat, the silica minerals in this fossilized tree turned to agate. Most of the tree's structure was destroyed.

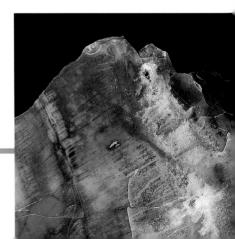

Crawling on Land

Top: A modern scorpion is similar to the first animals to walk on land.

Above: Insects first appeared 350 million years ago. This beetle was alive much later.

It was probably as difficult for animals to come out of the water and live on land as it was for plants. Animals had to change from breathing water to breathing air.

Animals that looked like scorpions may have been the first to live on land about 410 million years ago. They had lived in the oceans for millions of years, and some grew to nearly 10 feet (3 m) in length. Much later, huge dragonflies, over 3 feet (1 m) from wingtip to wingtip, flew above the forests of the Carboniferous Period.

Insects make up the largest group of animals on our planet today. Unfortunately, few animal fossils from very early times remain to show what the early land creatures were like.

Below: A fossil cranefly from the early Cenozoic Period is almost identical to the craneflies of today.

Huge dragonflies, with the same shape as this modern one, flew during Carboniferous times.

From looking at fossils of fish, it is possible to see how some fish fins could have gradually changed to short legs. These first land vertebrates, or animals with backbones, emerged from water about 360 million years ago. The animals were similar to modern-day newts and salamanders.

Fish with leglike fins still exist today. They are called mudskippers. At low tide, they drag themselves out of the water and over the mud with their front fins. They can even climb trees!

Above: A modern-day mudskipper uses its front fins like legs.

Left: Fish that once walked on their fins became four-footed animals. They must have looked like today's axolotl salamanders.

21

Living Fossils

Top: The modern ginkgo is the only species left of the many different ginkgo species that once existed.

Above: These ginkgo leaf impressions were formed during Permian times. During that period, ginkgoes flourished throughout the world.

Right: Today's horseshoe crabs may have descended from trilobites.

Throughout the world, the fossilized remains of ginkgo trees are found in the same rock layers as dinosaur fossils. Fossil ginkgo leaves are the same shape as the leaves of today's ginkgo trees. The ginkgo has somehow managed to survive unchanged during the 65 million years since the age of dinosaurs. It is a living fossil.

There are many other examples of living fossils. Ancient-looking, armored horseshoe crabs live on the eastern coast of North America. They are closely related to the Silurian horseshoe crabs that lived 430 million years ago.

Amazingly, these crabs have lived on, unchanged, all that time. In addition, horseshoe crab **larvae** look like the long-extinct trilobites. This means that horseshoe crabs may well have descended from trilobites.

Left: This illustration of an archaeopteryx — the "first bird"— is based on fossil evidence. It had feathers like today's birds, but it also had teeth.

It is safe to say there are no dinosaur living fossils. But close descendants of the dinosaurs live on. There is fossil evidence that small dinosaurs that ran on their hind legs began to use their front legs as wings. These dinosaurs evolved into birds. Even fossil dinosaur eggs are very similar to birds' eggs. So perhaps the dinosaurs did not entirely become extinct. Some **evolved** into birds that fly all around us!

Above: These are actual fossilized dinosaur eggs. The dinosaurs have disappeared, but their distant relations — birds — live on.

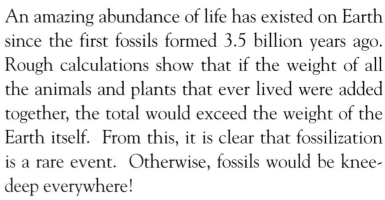

Gone Forever

Top: The Silurian oceans seethed with trilobites.

Opposite: Mysterious trilobites, like this fossilized one from Ordovician times, crawled over the seabed on many legs.

Below: Hundreds of species of ammonites lived during **Triassic** times. Today, not a single species survives.

Below: The pearly nautilus is the nearest living relative of the ammonites.

An amazing abundance of life has existed on Earth since the first fossils formed 3.5 billion years ago. Rough calculations show that if the weight of all the animals and plants that ever lived were added together, the total would exceed the weight of the Earth itself. From this, it is clear that fossilization is a rare event. Otherwise, fossils would be knee-deep everywhere!

Countless animal and plant species have existed over time. The millions of species alive today are just a tiny fraction of the total number of species that the Earth has seen. Most species became extinct long ago.

Trilobites are a good example of a type of animal that was very successful at one time but eventually became extinct. Once, there were about a thousand species of trilobites. None survived beyond the Carboniferous Period, 290 million years ago. Trilobites may have been slow and easy for larger animals to catch for a meal. Fossils show that some species of trilobites could curl themselves up. This may have been their way of trying to defend themselves.

In the end, perhaps the larger animals eventually became too clever at catching and eating trilobites, forcing them into extinction.

Above: A fossil dinosaur bone from Jurassic times is evidence of these great reptiles that are now gone forever.

Some of the greatest animals that ever lived on Earth have become extinct. For 150 million years, from the Triassic Period to the Cretaceous, dinosaurs ruled the world. There were hundreds of species. They ranged in size from that of a rabbit to the monstrous sauropods that were nearly 100 feet (30 m) from nose to tip of the tail. Dinosaur fossils are found all over the world in layers of rock.

Above Cretaceous rocks, no dinosaur fossils are found. This shows that many of these great animals died out at the same time. No one knows exactly why, but one possibility is a huge meteorite strike that would have led to the elimination of the dinosaurs' food supply.

When many species die out at the same time, it is called a **mass extinction**. The distribution of fossils in rock layers shows that mass extinctions

Right: Huge dinosaurs, like these horned Styracosauruses, flourished in the millions during Jurassic and Cretaceous times. By the end of the Cretaceous Period, they had all disappeared.

have occasionally occurred. They may have been caused by huge volcanic eruptions or by giant meteorites or comets colliding with Earth. These events would have sent up massive ash and dust into the atmosphere, blocking the Sun and causing darkness and bitter cold for a long time.

Today, overpopulation of humans on Earth is causing a mass extinction of plants and animals that is probably greater than any mass extinction that occurred in the past.

Above: Some ancient reptiles that walked on land later went back to the water. Their legs changed to flippers, and their tails developed fins. They became Ichthyosaurs that lived during Jurassic times, all now extinct.

Some small dinosaurs survived extinction by evolving feathers and wings and becoming birds.

Activities:

Finding Fossils

You do not have to be an expert to find fossils. They are easy to find if you know where to look. The first thing to realize is that fossils occur only in sedimentary rocks.

Sedimentary rocks are laid down in layers — layers of sediment at the bottom of lakes and seawaters, layers of volcanic ash, layers of wind-blown sand, or even layers of peat. Rocks formed in volcanoes do not contain fossils. These rocks were very hot and deep underground when they formed. No living things could have been preserved in them. Even some sedimentary rocks, such as marble, have become changed by heat and pressure so that any fossils that once were in them have been destroyed. So it is important to learn to recognize the right type of rocks.

Cliffs and Quarries

Some of the best places to look for fossils are where rocks are breaking away from cliffs. When waves pound against the shore, pieces of rock may break off, exposing fossils. The waves tumble the pieces, grinding them slowly away. Then, the fossils inside the rock can be seen.

Old quarries are also good places for fossil hunting. No wave action occurs in old quarries to expose the fossils. The cliffs are humanmade.

Before you start on a fossil-hunting expedition, you will need (see above): a hammer, chisel, notebook, pencil, magnifying glass, paper towels, a pair of goggles, and a bag. If the area you search has high, steep cliffs, you will also need a hard hat and an adult along to supervise. The bag is for carrying your fossil-hunting gear and any specimens you may find.

Your Eyes Only

Search along the base of a cliff (left) for fossils. You will soon discover which rock layers have fossils and which do not.

Choose a small chunk of rock with a few fossils showing on the outside and try splitting it with hammer and chisel. Rest your chisel on the edge of the rock, in line with the layers. Then, with the help of an adult, carefully give the rock a sharp tap with the hammer. Wear goggles when doing this because pieces of rock can fly off.

It is very exciting when the rock splits neatly into two pieces, and you find a fossil that has been sandwiched inside for millions of years!

If a fossil is worth collecting, wrap it in a piece of paper towel along with a slip of paper saying where and when you found it.

Store your fossil collection in boxes in a suitable cabinet or drawer. Make sure your labels stay with the right specimens. You may be able to identify the fossils later and then estimate the age of the rocks where you found them.

Making an Impression

To see how a fossil impression forms, you will need a flat leaf, some thin cardboard, a paper clip, Vaseline, plaster of paris, and a container to mix the plaster in.

Cut a strip of cardboard about 1 inch (3 centimeters) wide, and bend it into a round shape that will surround the leaf with a little room to spare (*below*). Secure the ends of the cardboard strip with the paper clip. Place the circle of cardboard on an old plate. Mix enough plaster of paris to fill half the circle, and pour the thick, creamy mixture in.

Smooth the surface of the plaster and place the leaf on it. Gently press the leaf to get rid of bubbles.

When the plaster hardens, smear a very thin layer of Vaseline over the plaster surface, trying not to get too much of it on the leaf. Now mix the same amount of plaster again, and pour it on top of the leaf. This is like sediment falling onto the leaf. When the second layer of plaster hardens, remove the cardboard and carefully pry the two layers of plaster apart. Remove the leaf (*above*). You now have two halves of a leaf impression, just as the leaf might have fossilized in sedimentary rock.

Glossary

ammonite: a sea creature with a coiled shell that lived millions of years ago.

bivalve: an animal with a shell made of two separate halves.

calcium carbonate: a chemical formed of calcium, carbon, and oxygen.

Cambrian: the period in prehistory 550 to 510 million years ago.

Carboniferous: the period in prehistory 353 to 290 million years ago.

Cenozoic: the last 65 million years of prehistory.

Cretaceous: the period in prehistory 146 to 65 million years ago.

cyanobacteria: a group of microscopic organisms that live in water.

evolved: advanced gradually over time.

extinct: no longer existing on Earth.

flint: a type of hard, brittle rock made of silica.

geologist: a person who studies geology, the science of rocks.

growth rings: patterns in tree trunks, fish scales, and other hard parts of animals that form as growth speeds and slows.

impression: the shape left by an object pressed into soft material.

index fossil: a fossil species used by geologists to determine the age of rocks.

Jurassic: the period in prehistory 205 to 146 million years ago.

larvae (*plural*): the early form of animals.

limestone: medium-hard rock formed of calcium carbonate by heat and pressure.

mass extinction: a period when many species become extinct during a relatively short span of time.

mineral: a simple chemical found in soil.

peat: material formed of the compressed stems and leaves of plants long dead.

prehistoric: occurring before events were recorded by humans.

resin: sticky sap that oozes from the trunks and branches of some plants, particularly conifers.

sediment: material that sinks to the bottom of rivers, lakes, oceans, and seas.

sedimentary: the name for rocks that have been formed by the settling of natural materials. Sedimentary rocks always build layers.

silica: a compound of silicon and oxygen called silicon dioxide.

silt: fine particles suspended in or deposited from water.

spicules: microscopic, needle-like crystals of silica or calcium carbonate that make up the skeletons of sponges.

stromatolite: a rounded mound formed by the fossils of cyanobacteria.

Triassic: the period in prehistory 251 to 205 million years ago.

trilobite: an extinct animal with a jointed body and many legs that lived on Earth 550 to 290 million years ago.

Plants and Animals

The common names of plants and animals vary from language to language. But plants and animals also have scientific names, based on Greek or Latin words, that are the same the world over. Each plant and animal has two scientific names. The first name is called the genus. It starts with a capital letter. The second name is the species name. It starts with a small letter.

ammonite (*Echioceras raricostatum*) — England 8; (*Dactyloceras commune*) — Triassic, England 24

archaeopteryx (*Archaeopteryx lithographica*) — Jurassic, Europe 23

axolotl (*Siredon mexicanum*) — present day, Mexico 21

cranefly (*Tipula spoliata*) — Cenozoic, North America 20

fish fossil (*Leptolepis sprattiformes*) — Jurassic, Europe 4-5

fly (*Plecia pealei*) — Cenozoic, North America 7

ginkgo (*Ginkgo biloba*) — China, planted elsewhere 22

ginkgo fossil (*Ginkgo huttoni*) — Cenozoic, England 22

heart urchin (*Micraster coranguinum*) — Cretaceous, worldwide 14, 15

horseshoe crab (*Tachypleus gigas*) — western Pacific coasts 22

lamp shells (*Calcirhynchia calcaria*) — England 7

mackerel shark (*Carcharocles megalodon*) — Cenozoic, worldwide 7

mammoth (*Mammuthus primigenius*) — Cenozoic, Europe 11

mudskipper (*Periophthalmus barbarus*) — tropical shores 21

pearly nautilus (*Nautilus pompilius*) — southern Pacific Ocean 24

scorpion (*Urodacus novae-hollandii*) — present, Australia 20

sea lily (*Pentacrinites fossilis*) — Jurassic, Europe, North America 16

shark (Odontaspis) — Cenozoic, France 5

sponge (*Siphonia koenigi*) — Cretaceous, England 14, 15

tree fossil (*Dadoxylon alberi*) — Carboniferous, Africa 10

trilobite (*Calymene blumenbachi*) — Silurian, England 24

Books to Read

Death Trap: The Story of the La Brea Tar Pits. Sharon E. Thompson (Lerner)
Digging Up Tyrannosaurus Rex. Jack Horner and Don Lessem (Crown Books for Young Readers)
Extinct Species (series). (Gareth Stevens)
Fossil Detective. Joyce Pope (Troll)
Fossils. Carol Bernanti (Random Books)

Fossils. Douglas Palmer (Dorling Kindersley)
Fossils. William Russell (Rourke)
Fossils of the World. Chris Pellant (Thunder Bay Press)
The New Dinosaur Collection (series). (Gareth Stevens)
World of Dinosaurs (series). (Gareth Stevens)

Videos and Web Sites

Videos

Digging Dinosaurs. (Centre Communications)
Dinosaurs. (Instructional Video)
The Fossil Rush — Tale of a Bone. (Arts & Entertainment Network)
Fossils. (Film Ideas, Inc.)
Fossils. (Instructional Video)
Fossils! Fossils! (Barr Films)

Web Sites

members.aol.com/dinoprints/index.html
home.earthlink.net/~skurth/
www.PSIAZ.com/Schur/azpaleo.html
cadvantage.com/~leiszler/
www.narcy.com/fossils
www.terracom.net/~mcm/fossil.html
www.wa.nea.org/INFO/Orgnztn/ TCHGPAST.HTM

Some web sites stay current longer than others. For further web sites, use your search engines to locate the following topics: *dinosaurs, extinction, fossils, geology, prehistory,* and *rocks.*

Index

amber 9
ammonites 8, 12, 24
archaeopteryx 23

bivalves 16

calcium carbonate 14, 16
Cambrian Period 12, 13
Carboniferous Period 10, 13, 20, 24
Cenozoic Era 9, 10, 13, 20
chalk rock 14, 15
Cretaceous Period 6, 9, 13, 14, 26
cyanobacteria 12

Devonian Period 8, 13
dinosaurs 6, 9, 22, 23, 26, 27

extinction 8, 9, 24, 26, 27

flint 14, 15

geologic time scale 13
growth rings 18

impressions 8, 9, 11, 22
index fossils 12

Jurassic Period 6, 12, 13, 16, 26, 27

limestone 16, 17

mammoths 11
mass extinctions 26, 27
minerals 4-5, 7

Ordovician Period 13, 24-25

Permian Period 13, 22

resin 9

sediment 14
sedimentary rock 7
silica 15, 19
silt 5, 14
Silurian Period 13, 22, 24
spicules 15
stromatolites 12

Triassic Period 13, 24, 26
trilobites 12, 22, 24-25

vertebrates 21